★ 50 WORDS ★
ABOUT NATURE
ANIMALS

LILY HOLLAND

DEBBIE POWELL

OXFORD
UNIVERSITY PRESS

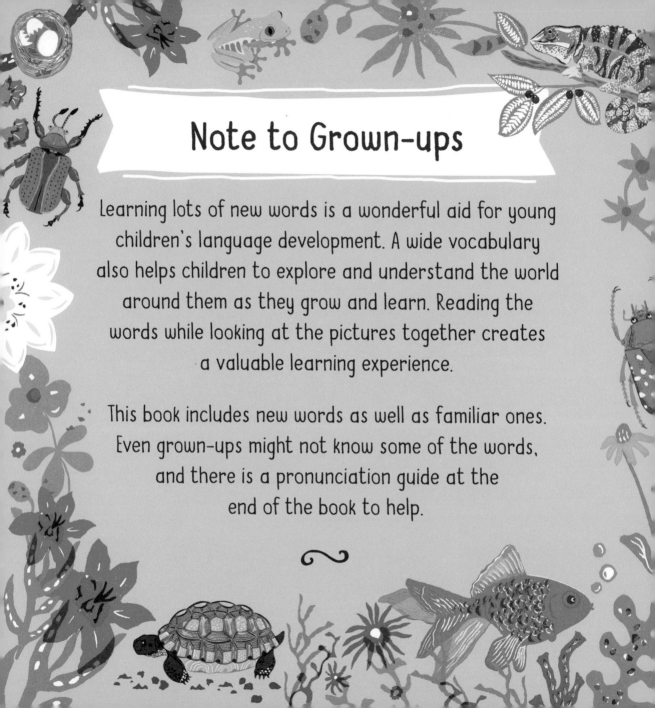

Note to Grown-ups

Learning lots of new words is a wonderful aid for young children's language development. A wide vocabulary also helps children to explore and understand the world around them as they grow and learn. Reading the words while looking at the pictures together creates a valuable learning experience.

This book includes new words as well as familiar ones. Even grown-ups might not know some of the words, and there is a pronunciation guide at the end of the book to help.

In this book you will find **50 words** about **animals**, which are living things just like you. There are lots and lots of different kinds. Keep reading to find out about some of the most **interesting** animals on **Earth**.

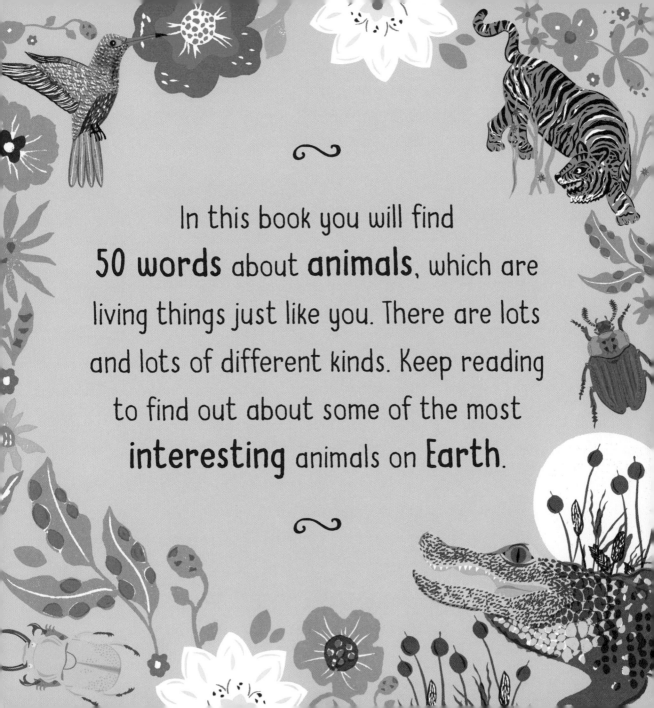

Birds are animals that have:

two **wings**

a **beak**

two legs

All birds are covered in **feathers**. This one is a **hummingbird**.

Baby birds, like this chick, hatch from **eggs** laid by their mother.

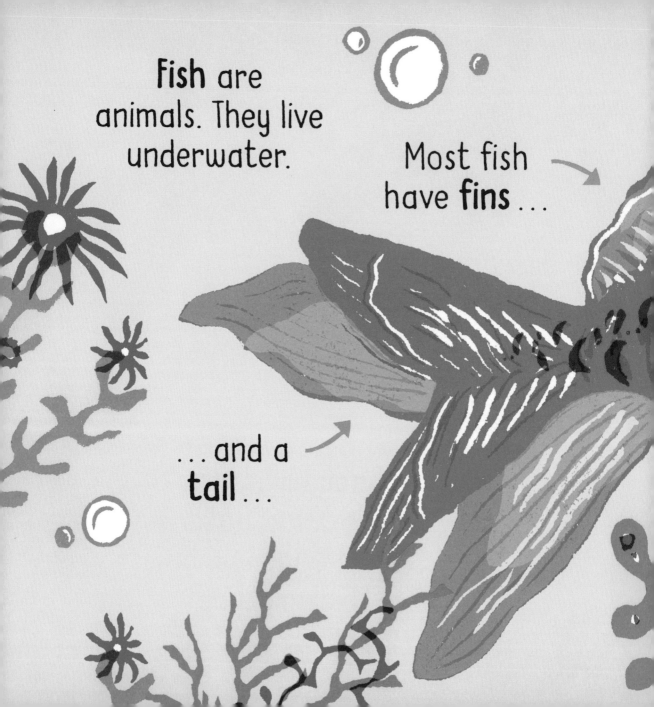

Fish are animals. They live underwater.

Most fish have **fins**...

...and a **tail**...

...and are covered in **scales**, like this **goldfish**.

Fish breathe through **gills**.

Reptiles are **cold-blooded** animals, which means they need heat from the sun to warm them up.

Alligators are a type of reptile.

Alligators live in rivers, lakes, marshes and swamps.

Different kinds of animal are
called different **species**.

There are thousands
of species of reptile.

Some, like this **tortoise**, have hard
shells on their backs for protection.

Most reptiles have scales.

This **chameleon** can change colour.

This **red-eyed tree frog** is an amphibian.

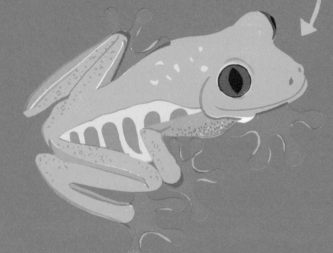

It has damp skin and lives both on land and in water.

Frogs lay eggs called **frogspawn**.

The eggs hatch into **tadpoles**, which live underwater.

Then they grow legs
and become frogs.

Mammals are **warm-blooded**. Their bodies can make their own heat to keep warm.

There are lots of species of mammal.

Marine mammals, like this **dolphin**, live in the ocean.

They need to come to the surface to breathe air.

Some animals eat other animals—
they are **carnivores**.

This **tiger** is
hunting a **deer**.

The tiger is
a **predator**
and the deer
is its **prey**.

The deer is a **herbivore**, which means it only eats plants.

Animals that eat both plants and animals are **omnivores**.

This **gorilla** is an **ape**.

Monkeys and apes are called **primates**, which are animals with forward-facing eyes, and hands with fingers that are good at holding things.

Humans are also primates.

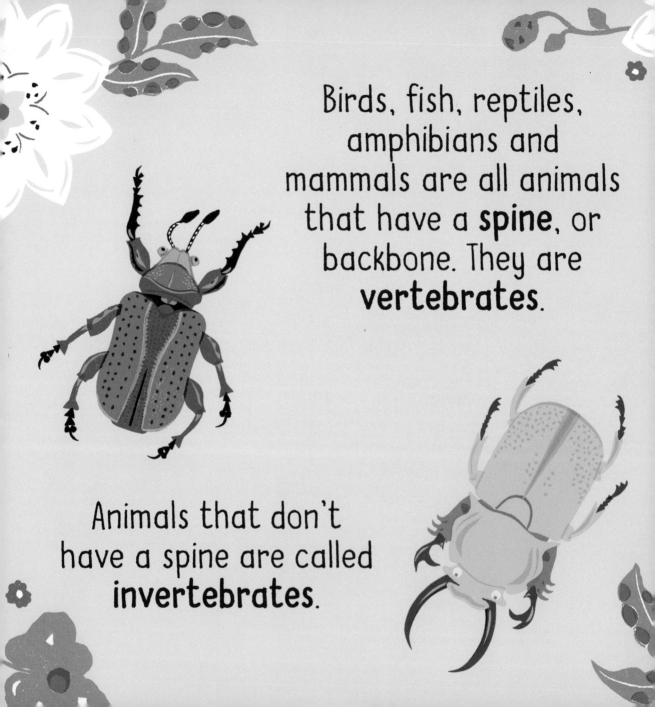

Birds, fish, reptiles, amphibians and mammals are all animals that have a **spine**, or backbone. They are **vertebrates**.

Animals that don't have a spine are called **invertebrates**.

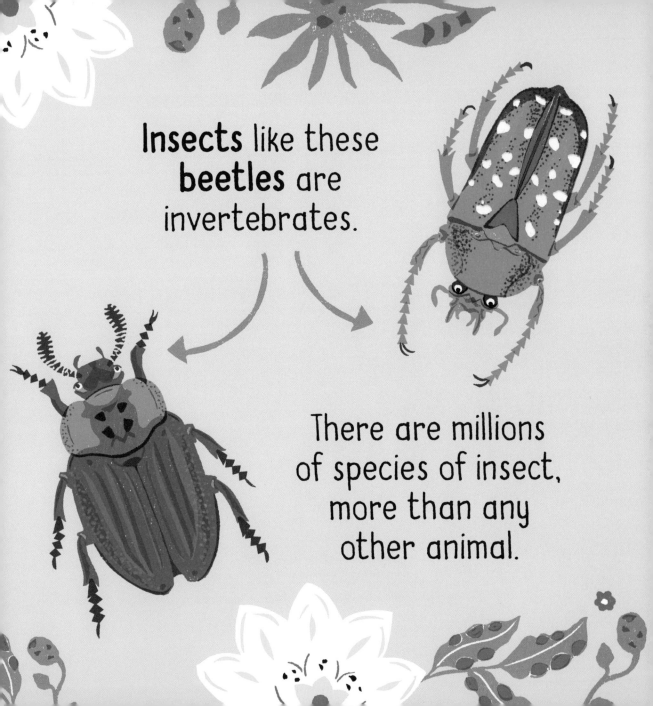

Insects like these **beetles** are invertebrates.

There are millions of species of insect, more than any other animal.

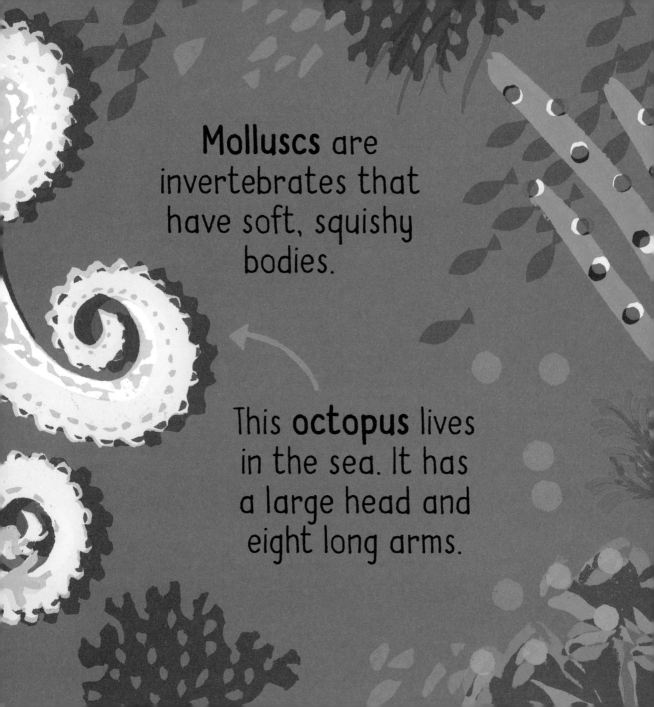

Molluscs are invertebrates that have soft, squishy bodies.

This **octopus** lives in the sea. It has a large head and eight long arms.

The place where an animal lives is called its **habitat**.

Animals that are in danger of becoming extinct are called endangered species.

Some animals have become **extinct**. This means that all of that species has died out.

This **bactrian camel** is an endangered species that lives in a desert habitat.

One way of protecting endangered animals is by looking after their habitats.

People who
study animals
are called
zoologists.

They learn about how
animals live, and how we
can help to save
endangered species.

shark

tail

You could be like a zoologist and learn more about your favourite animals.

Do you know what kind of habitat they live in?

eagle

camouflage

How many other words about animals do you know?

wingspan